Published by Red Panda, an imprint of Westland Books, a division of Nasadiya Technologies Private Limited, in 2025

No. 269/2B, First Floor, 'Irai Arul', Vimalraj Street, Nethaji Nagar, Alapakkam Main Road, Maduravoyal, Chennai 600095

Westland, the Westland logo, Red Panda and the Red Panda logo are the trademarks of Nasadiya Technologies Private Limited, or its affiliates.

Copyright © Nasadiya Technologies Private Limited, 2025

Images sourced from Shutterstock

ISBN: 9789371972406

10 9 8 7 6 5 4 3 2 1

All rights reserved

Printed at Nutech Print Services, India

No part of this book may be reproduced, or stored in a retrieval system, or transmitted in any form or by any means, electronic, mechanical, photocopying, recording, or otherwise, without express written permission of the publisher.

HISTORIC MOMENT

On the night of 14 August 1947, India's first Prime Minister, Jawaharlal Nehru, stood before the Constituent Assembly at Parliament House and delivered his famous 'Tryst with Destiny' speech.
Can you spot the differences between these two images?

DID YOU KNOW? Since this speech was delivered just before midnight India celebrates Independence Day on 15 August 1947!

HISTORY MIX-UP

Can you match each historic event to the right date? Read the clues carefully!

MON	TUE	WED	THU	FRI	SAT	SUN
1	2 October	3	4	5	6	7
8	9	10	11	12 March 1930	13	14 April
15 August 1947	16	17	18	19	20	21
22	23	24 September 2014	25	26 January 1950	27	28
29	30	31				

A India gained independence from British rule after nearly 200 years.
....

B India became a Republic.
....

D Birthday of India's peace-loving freedom fighter.
....

C India's first Mars mission, *Mangalyaan*, blasts off!
....

E A historic protest against the British salt tax.
....

MISSION MANGAL

The *Mangalyaan* mission had many important moments. Fill in the blanks with missing dates or events.

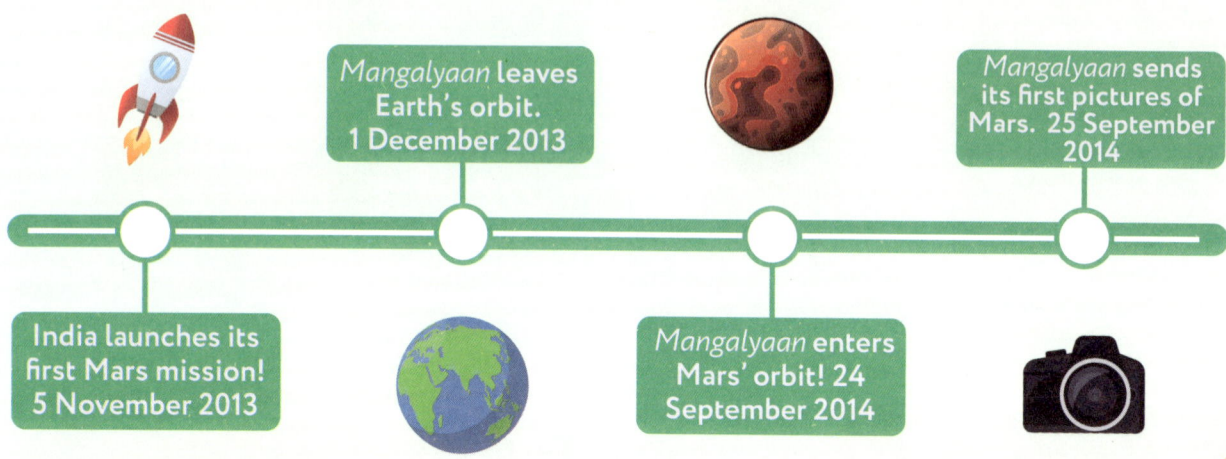

Timeline with Blanks

1. _____: *Mangalyaan* was launched from ISRO's space centre.

2. _____ : The spacecraft left Earth's orbit and started its journey to Mars.

3. 24 September 2014: _____

4. _____ : *Mangalyaan* sent its first images of Mars to Earth.

DID YOU KNOW? *Mangalyaan* was the first mission in the world to reach Mars on the very first try! And guess what? It cost less than the Hollywood movie Gravity!

TRICOLOUR TIME TRAVEL

Colour the first flag of India that was unfurled on 7 August 1906, during the protest against British rule. Can you use the right colours for the stripes and the symbols?

5

RULE THE REPUBLIC!

India's Constitution came into effect in 1950, and our country became a republic—which means we began following rules made by the people, for the people. Read each fun fact and tell if it's True or False?

	True	False

1. The Indian Constitution was adopted on 26 January 1950.
2. Republic Day is celebrated on the anniversary of India's independence from British rule.
3. The first Republic Day parade took place in 1947.
4. The President of India unfurls the national flag during the Republic Day ceremony.
5. The Republic Day celebrations last for one day only.
6. The Republic Day parade showcases India's military strength and cultural diversity.
7. The first Republic Day parade took place without a chief guest.
8. Jawaharlal Nehru drafted the Constitution of India.
9. Republic Day marks the day India became independent.
10. India's Republic Day is a national holiday in all states of India.

THE CROP CALCULATOR

The Green Revolution began in the 1960s and transformed farming across India. Farmers started using high-yield varieties of wheat and rice. Imagine you're a farmer. You grow wheat in three sections of your field and rice in five and each section produces 50 kg of wheat and 40 kg of rice.

Now, let's calculate the total food production!
How much wheat does the farmer produce in total?
What is the total amount of food the farmer produces from both wheat and rice?

DID YOU KNOW? The high-yield varieties of wheat and rice introduced during the Green Revolution could produce up to 10 times more food than traditional crop varieties, making it a game-changer for global food security.

A SPECIAL CARD FOR MY TEACHER!

5 September is Teacher's Day in India, a day to celebrate the amazing teachers who guide us, inspire us and help us grow.

Write a heartfelt message for your teacher.

Draw a picture of you and your teacher together.

DID YOU KNOW? Teacher's Day in India is celebrated on 5 September, the birthday of Dr. Radhakrishnan, a great teacher and India's second President.

THE HIMALAYAN ADVENTURE

On 20 May 1965, India made mountaineering history! Sonam Gyatso and Nawang S. S. became the first Indians to climb Mount Everest, the tallest mountain in the world. Observe these two images and spot four differences.

DID YOU KNOW? Mount Everest grows taller every year! Due to shifting tectonic plates, the mountain rises by about 4 millimetres annually.

DANDI MARCH DETOUR

On 12 March 1930, Mahatma Gandhi began the Salt March—a peaceful walk from Sabarmati to Dandi to protest the unfair salt tax. Help him reach the sea! Find the right path through the maze, but watch out ... some routes are blocked by British soldiers!

DID YOU KNOW? When Gandhiji reached the seashore, he picked up a handful of salt and declared, 'With this, I am shaking the foundations of the British Empire.' This inspired millions to join the freedom movement!

ROLE MODELS

National Girl Child Day, celebrated on 24 January, is a reminder to appreciate the power, wisdom and potential of every girl and woman.

Think about five women who are very special to you. They could be your mom, grandma, teacher, aunt, friend, or even someone famous you admire.

WOMEN'S DAY WHO'S WHO

On International Women's Day, March 8, match the women achievers to their achievements.

INDIRA GANDHI

1. She was the first Indian-born woman to go to space. She flew aboard the Space Shuttle Columbia.

KIRAN BEDI

2. She founded the Missionaries of Charity and won the Nobel Peace Prize. She devoted her life to helping the poor, sick and needy.

BARKHA DUTT

3. She was the first female Prime Minister of India and led the country for over a decade.

KALPANA CHAWLA

4. A leading Indian journalist and television personality, she rose to fame for her coverage of the Kargil War and became a prominent voice in Indian media.

MOTHER TERESA

5. The first female officer in the Indian Police Service (IPS), she broke barriers by becoming the first woman to join the force.

THE CRICKET CONUNDRUM

India won its first Cricket World Cup on 25 June 1983. Solve these math puzzles to answer questions related to Indian cricket.

1. India needs 36 runs to win in the last 6 overs with 4 wickets left. What is the required run rate per over?

Formula: Required run rate = Runs needed ÷ Overs left

Answer: ....

2. If a bowler delivers 4 maiden overs in a 10-over spell and concedes 40 runs, what is his economy rate?

Formula: Economy rate = Runs conceded ÷ Overs bowled

Answer: ....

3. In a T20 match, a team scores 200 runs in 20 overs. How many runs per over did they score on average?

Formula: Runs per over = Total runs ÷ Overs faced

Answer: ....

4. A cricketer hit 6 sixes, 5 fours and 2 doubles. How many runs did he score?

Answer: ....

5. A bowler takes 5 wickets in 10 overs while conceding 30 runs. What is his bowling average?

Formula: Bowling average = Runs conceded ÷ Wickets taken

Answer: ....

DID YOU KNOW? Kapil Dev, India's legendary cricketer, was the first player to take 400 wickets in One-Day Internationals? He achieved this milestone in 1994 and his all-round performances played a crucial role in India's success in the 1983 World Cup!

YOGA FOR HEALTH

International Yoga Day is celebrated every year on 21 June! Look at the different yoga poses below and match each pose to its correct name.

1. Vrikshasana (Tree Pose)

A ○

2. Downward Dog

B ○

3. Padmasana (Lotus Pose)

C ○

4. Virabhadrasana (Warrior Pose)

D ○

5. Balasana (Child's Pose)

E ○

DID YOU KNOW? The word yoga comes from the Sanskrit word Yuj, which means to unite. Yoga helps to unite the body, mind and spirit for overall well-being!

THE GREAT STATE CHASE!

National Youth Day, on 12 January, celebrates the birthday of Swami Vivekananda, inspiring youth across India. Today, India has 28 states and 8 union territories. Some of them are already labelled on the map. Can you use the clues to name the missing states?

On 15 January, this southern state celebrates Pongal — a harvest festival filled with colourful kolams and sugarcane. Shaped like a boot, it lies in the south of India.
→ State: _____

On 2 October, this state celebrates Mahatma Gandhi's birth anniversary in Porbandar, his hometown. It's in western India.
→ State: _____

The statehood day of this Himalayan region is celebrated on 2 March. It's known for its snowy peaks and is home to the Dalai Lama, who lives here in exile.
→ State: _____

On 1 November, this lush state celebrates its Formation Day. It's known for its backwaters and palm-fringed beaches.
→ State: _____

On 1 November, this big central state also celebrates its Formation Day. It's called the 'Heart of India' because of its location.
→ State: _____

DID YOU KNOW? India has over 2,000 distinct languages, yet we are united as one nation.

THE SECRET ARMY MESSAGE

On 15 January 1949, Field Marshal K. M. Cariappa became the first Indian Commander-in-Chief of the Indian Army. Since then, we celebrate Indian Army Day on 15 January, every year, to remember this important change in India's history. During missions, the Indian Army uses secret codes to send messages securely. Can you decode this message?

4 - 9 - 14 - 4 - 9 - 1

Clue: Each number represents a letter. A = 1, B = 2, C = 3)

....

DID YOU KNOW? The Parachute Regiment (Special Forces) of the Indian Army is known for its extreme bravery and top-secret missions!

SPOT THE SPICES!

Indian Food Day is celebrated on 24 March to enjoy and learn about the many diverse flavours of Indian cuisine. Take a close look at the two pictures of an Indian kitchen filled with delicious food. Can you spot the differences between them?

DID YOU KNOW? India is home to more than 80 types of spices! These spices not only enhance the taste of food but also have medicinal properties!

INDIA'S JOURNEY TO FREEDOM

India's road to freedom was marked by struggles, sacrifices and historic milestones. Complete the timeline by adding the missing years and corresponding details.

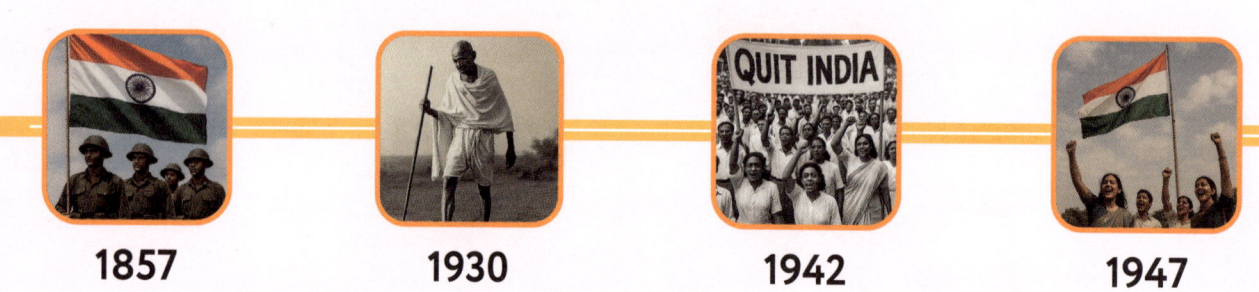

1857   1930   1942   1947

1. The First War of Indian Independence (also called the Sepoy Mutiny). _____

2. The Salt March was led by _____ (name the famous person)?

3. The Quit India Movement started with the slogan 'Do or Die,' given by _____.

4. India gains independence from British rule on _____.

FESTIVAL CONNECT

Match each festival to its correct date. Draw a line to connect them!

 REPUBLIC DAY 〇 〇 DECEMBER 25

 CHRISTMAS 〇 〇 JANUARY 14

 NATIONAL SCIENCE DAY 〇 〇 AUGUST 15

 CHILDREN'S DAY 〇 〇 JANUARY 26

 MAKAR SANKRANTI 〇 〇 FEBRUARY 28

 INDEPENDENCE DAY 〇 〇 NOVEMBER 14

EXPLORE INDIA

National Tourism Day is celebrated on 25 January every year. Name the tourist destinations marked on the map and answer the questions, on the next page.

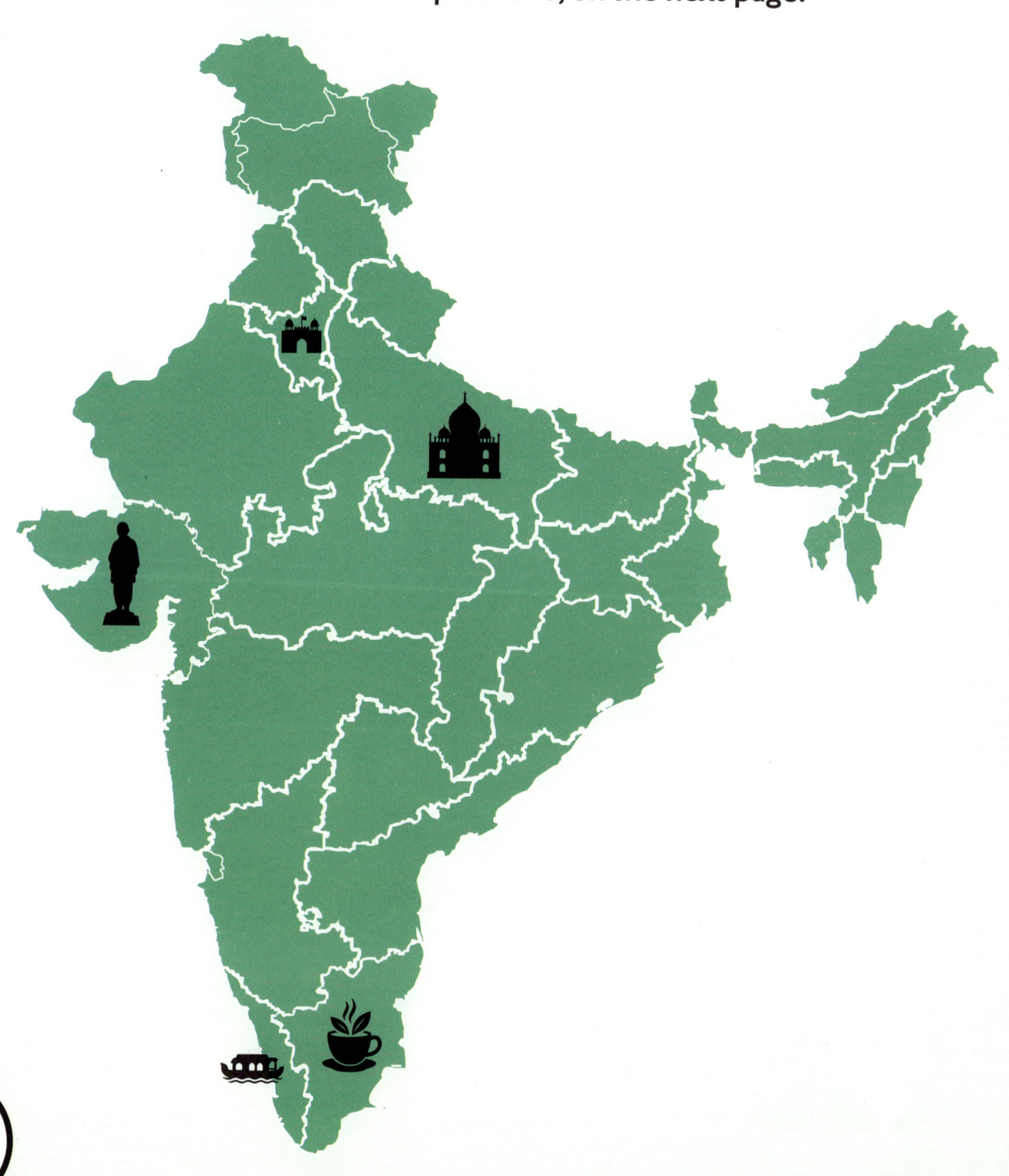

Built in 1653, this white marble monument is a symbol of love.
 (Hint: A famous mausoleum built by Emperor Shah Jahan)
→ Place: _____

Established as a hill station in the 19th century, this tea-filled spot in Tamil Nadu is called the Queen of Hills.
 (Hint: Popular for its toy train and cool weather)
→ Place: _____

This city has a Red Fort built in 1648 and many Mughal ruins.
→ Place: _____

This colourful city hosts a world-famous Camel Fair every November that attracts visitors from all over the world.
 (Hint: Located in Rajasthan and known for desert culture)
→ Place: _____

This city is home to the Statue of Unity, inaugurated on October 31, 2018, on Sardar Vallabhbhai Patel's birth anniversary.
 (Hint: Located in Gujarat)
→ Place: _____

In April every year, this spiritual city hosts the grand Ganga Aarti on the ghats of the Ganges River.
 (Hint: One of the oldest living cities in the world)
→ Place: _____

DID YOU KNOW? India has 40 UNESCO World Heritage Sites, making it a top destination for history and culture lovers!

MONUMENTAL TASK

From the Qutub Minar, built in 1193, to the Taj Mahal, completed in 1653, several Indian monuments are protected national treasures. Match the shadow of these monuments with their names.

1. Qutub Minar   O   O A

2. Red Fort   O   O B

3. Mysore Palace   O   O C

4. Gateway of India   O   O D

5. Taj Mahal   O   O E

DID YOU KNOW? The Qutub Minar in Delhi is the tallest brick minaret in the world! It stands at a height of 72.5 metres and was built in 1193.

NEHRU'S BIRTHDAY

Let's celebrate Jawaharlal Nehru's birthday on 14 November with some fun maths puzzles! He was born in 1889—and we'll use that number for some cool calculations. Can you crack these Nehru-themed challenges?

1. How old was Jawahar Lal Nehru when he became Congress President at the historic Lahore session that called for Purna Swaraj?

Ans.............................

2. Nehru became Prime Minister in 1947. How many years passed between his birth and becoming the leader of India?

Ans.............................

3. Nehru passed away in 1964. How many years after his birth did he pass away?

Ans.............................

4. If Jawaharlal Nehru was born in 1889, how many years after his birth did the Indian Constitution come into effect in 1950?

Ans.............................

CREATE YOUR OWN FARM!

National Farmers' Day is celebrated on 4 December to honour the hardworking farmers who help feed the nation. Imagine you're a farmer and draw your farm. Also, write a short story about your day.

1. What crops do you grow? (Hint: Wheat, rice, vegetables or fruits!)

2. Do you have any animals on your farm? (Hint: Cow, hen, goat, sheep!)

3. What tools do you use on your farm? (Hint: Tractor, plough, watering can!)

4. Describe a typical day on the farm. (Hint: Do you wake up early? What tasks do you do first?)

Draw your farm.

DID YOU KNOW? India is one of the largest producers of rice, wheat and vegetables in the world. Indian farmers play a vital role in the economy.

MONUMENT MYSTERY

Solve these tricky riddles to discover some of India's most famous monuments. Can you match the right monument to each riddle?

1

A — I'm a victory gate that marked a king's return. What am I?

2

B — I have 365 jharokhas (windows), but no one lives inside me. What am I?

3

C — I change colours with the sun - sometimes pink, sometimes gold, sometimes white. What am I?

4

D — I am an iron pillar that never rusts, standing strong for over 1,600 years. What am I?

5

E — I am taller than a giraffe, but can't move an inch. What am I?

SARDAR PATEL'S CONTRIBUTION TO INDIA'S UNITY

National Unity Day is observed on 31 October to celebrate the birth anniversary of Sardar Vallabhbhai Patel, the leader who played a key role in uniting India's many princely states into one nation.
Can you unscramble the names of some of these princely states?

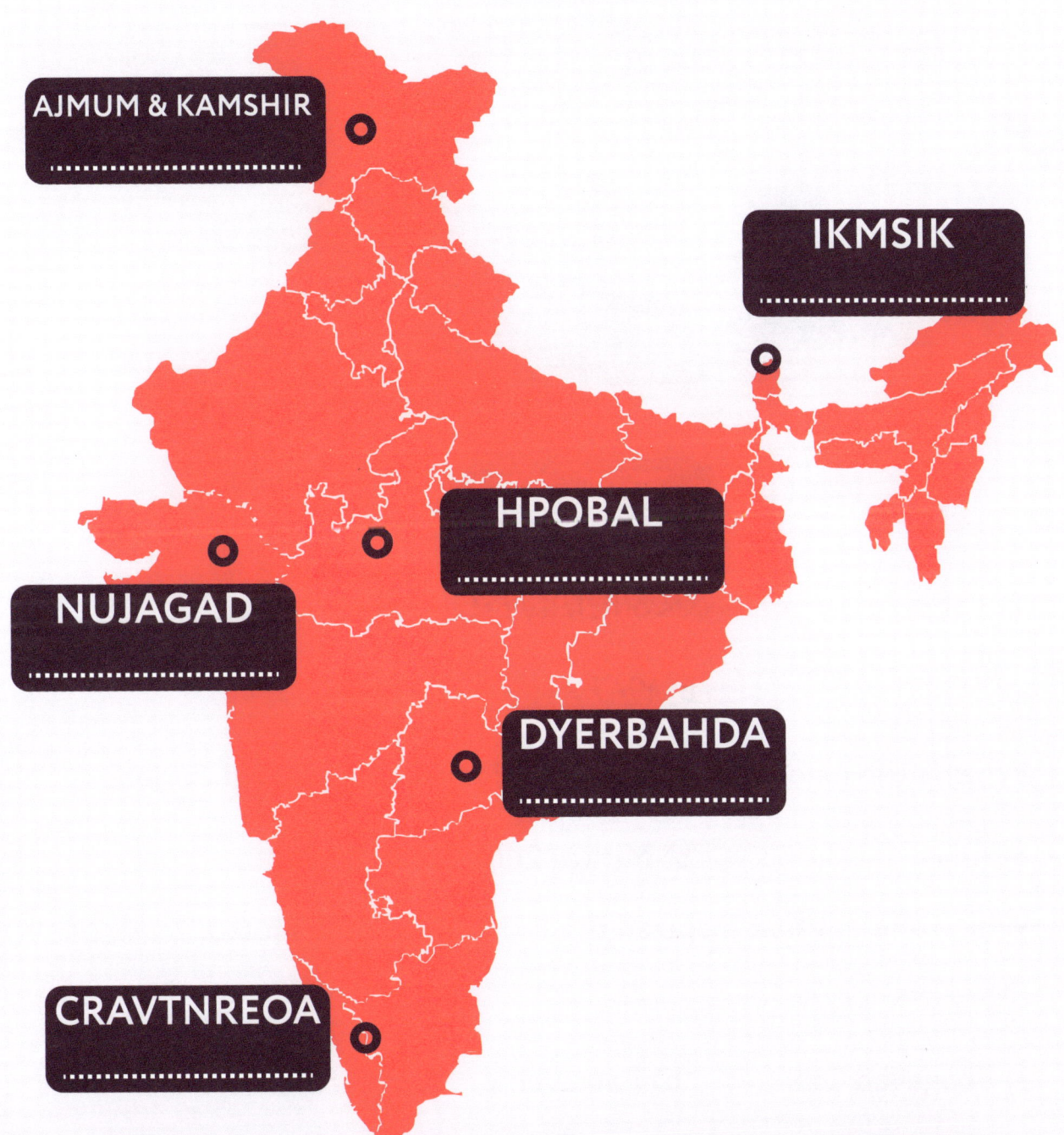

- AJMUM & KAMSHIR ....
- IKMSIK ....
- HPOBAL ....
- NUJAGAD ....
- DYERBAHDA ....
- CRAVTNREOA ....

DID YOU KNOW ? Sardar Patel is famously known as the Iron Man of India for his leadership and determination that shaped India's

SOARING HIGH

It's Indian Air Force Day on 8 October, a day to salute our sky warriors! Answer the questions below to keep soaring through history!

The Indian Air Force was officially established in _____ ?

a) 1932 b) 1947 c) 1950

What is the name of India's first indigenously built fighter jet?

a) Tejas b) Mirage 2000 c) Rafale

Which ancient text inspired the Indian Air Force motto, *Touch the Sky with Glory?*

a) Bhagavad Gita b) Ramayana c) Arthashastra

MISSION MOON

Chandrayaan-3 landed on the Moon on 23 August 2023. Find the words related to India's Moon mission hidden in the grid. Look carefully, they can go in any direction: horizontal, vertical or diagonal.

H	T	Y	K	V	R	O	V	E	R
L	O	F	E	G	Y	L	D	S	I
N	A	L	Z	T	G	O	J	D	X
I	E	R	E	D	N	A	L	N	S
T	N	A	Y	G	A	R	P	E	O
Q	M	O	O	N	O	V	G	A	R
V	I	Q	Z	Q	X	S	A	W	S
R	A	U	K	L	F	Z	Z	E	I
D	E	Q	J	U	C	N	W	X	K
H	Y	V	I	K	R	A	M	A	V

Moon   Lander
Rover   Vikram
Pragyan   ISRO

DID YOU KNOW? The *Chandrayaan-3* rover, Pragyan, left imprints of the ISRO logo and the Indian national emblem on the Moon's surface.

31

SHIP AHOY!

On Indian Navy Day, 4 December, draw your own battleship with features like radar, cannons, helicopters and a flag. Name it and colour it navy blue and get creative!

DID YOU KNOW ? The Indian Navy has its own special mascot – a dolphin! Dolphins are known for their intelligence and speed, which is why they are the perfect symbol for the Navy. The dolphin is also a sign of the Navy's commitment to protecting India's coastal waters!

CAPTAIN OF THE SEAS!

Now solve this Navy-themed crossword to test your knowledge about ships, sailors and the sea.

Word Bank

Across

4. Maritime security force under the Indian Navy
6. An Underwater vessel used for stealth operations
8. Navy ship designed for anti-submarine warfare

Down

1. Aircraft operations carried out by the Indian Navy
2. The Highest rank in the Indian Navy
3. Military installation for Navy ships and personnel
5. Underwater activity performed by Navy divers
7. Vessels used for combat in naval warfare

WHEN INDIA CELEBRATES!

Many states and communities celebrate their New Year in March–April. Match each festival to the right picture and write the correct date next to it!

Vishu (Kerala; 14 April)

Baisakhi (Punjab; 13 or 14 April)

Poila Boishakh (West Bengal; 14/15 April)

Gudi Padwa (Maharashtra; March/April)

Ugadi (Andhra Pradesh/Karnataka; March/April)

ASHOKA'S EDICTS

Emperor Ashoka ruled India from 268 to 232 BCE. Search the words from Ashoka's edicts hidden in the grid below. Look up, down, across and diagonally!

I	Z	M	R	G	E	U	S	A	F
J	O	R	A	H	T	U	R	T	X
D	A	S	M	I	H	A	K	A	M
V	D	Z	U	F	A	J	N	L	W
X	M	F	P	D	M	Q	S	P	B
V	U	K	G	W	A	L	V	M	F
R	O	E	P	T	Q	Z	P	K	E
N	E	R	E	S	P	E	C	T	O
B	P	E	A	C	E	N	L	U	B
O	J	S	S	E	N	D	N	I	K

PEACE   TRUTH

KINDNESS   RESPECT

LAW   AHIMSA

MARKET DAY

The Mauryan Empire was founded in 321 BCE by Chandragupta Maurya. Markets in that era were bustling with fascinating people. Look at the market scene and match each letter to the correct role.

Monk

Trader

Scribe

....

....

....

Guard

Water Carrier

....

....

HOW MILK CHANGED INDIA

In the 1970s, Dr Verghese Kurien led India's White Revolution and helped farmers produce more milk by improving cow care and teamwork. Number the pictures from 1 to 4 to show the correct order of events.

Happy families drinking fresh milk

A farmer feeding a cow

Milk being delivered to the market

Farmers working together with milk cans

1. ....

2. ....

3. ....

4. ....

WHAT HAPPENED FIRST?

These invasions and rulers are all mixed up! Read each one and check the year. Write numbers 1 to 5 in the circles to show the correct order, from first to last.

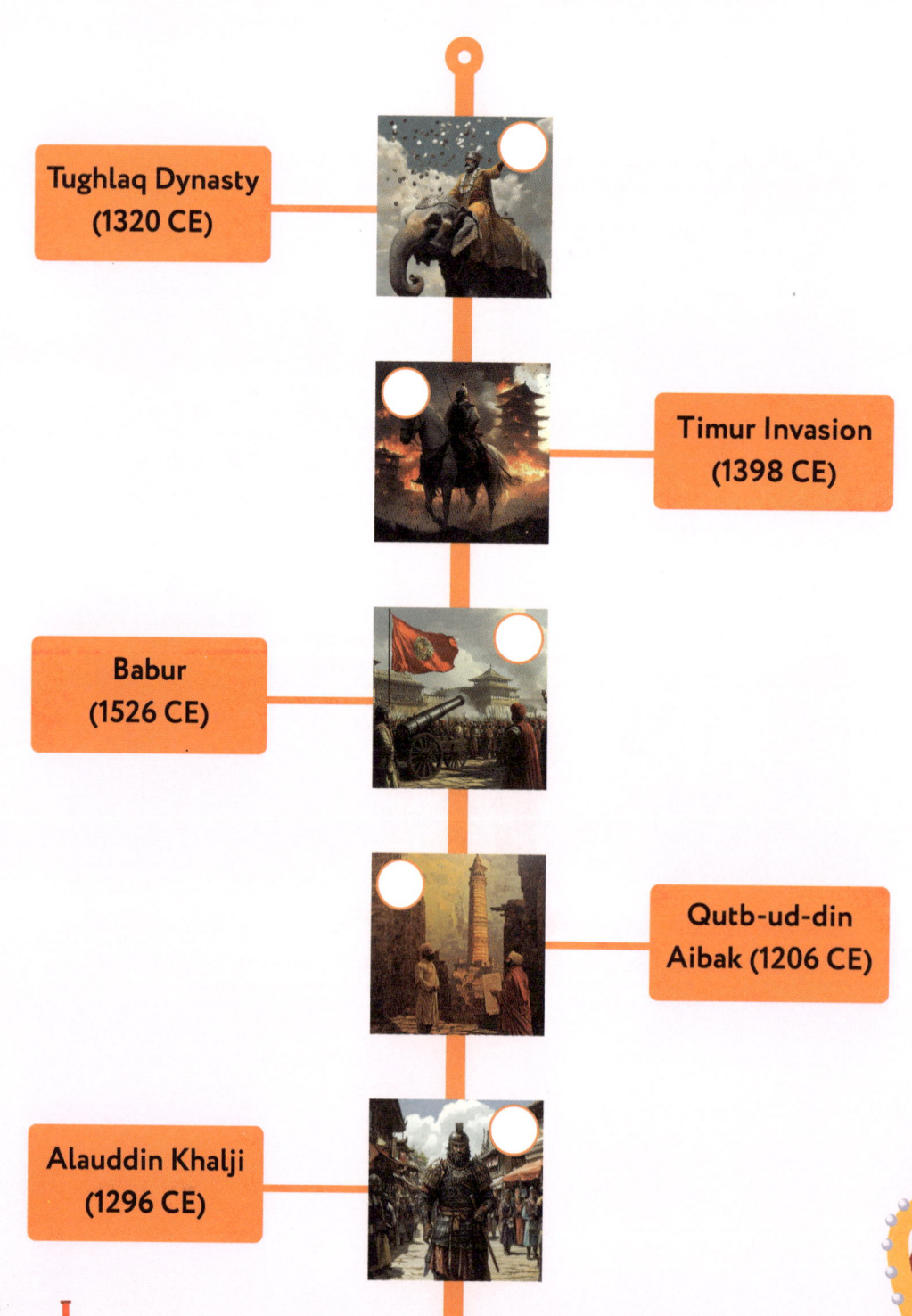

- Tughlaq Dynasty (1320 CE)
- Timur Invasion (1398 CE)
- Babur (1526 CE)
- Qutb-ud-din Aibak (1206 CE)
- Alauddin Khalji (1296 CE)

FREEDOM CELEBRATION

In 1961, Goa gained freedom after being ruled by the Portuguese for many years. Bring the moment to life by colouring the scene—the story of Goa's freedom!

THE SPINNING EARTH

Around 499 CE, mathematician Aryabhata, wrote the *Aryabhatiya*. He explained that the Earth spins, used maths to study the sky, helped shape how we count and gave the idea of zero. Observe the picture and answer the questions below:

Circle all the stars that have even numbers.

Count how many stars are in the sky. _____

Draw your own planet and give it a name Aryabhata would like.

DRAW YOUR OWN PLANET

MAHAVIRA'S NIRVANA

Help Light the Path to Peace! Lord Mahavira, the 24th Tirthankara of Jainism, attained nirvana (liberation) at the age of 72 in Pavapuri, Bihar, in 527 BCE. Colour the scene and draw five extra glowing lamps to show how Mahavira's teachings continue to shine in the world.

TIMELESS TALES

Match each emperor to the year and monument they're famous for. Study the silhouettes to make the correct match.

Babur ○   1526   ARAM BAGH, AGRA

Humayun ○   1648   TAJ MAHAL, AGRA

Akbar ○   1570   HUMAYUN'S TOMB, DELHI

Shah Jahan ○   1678   BIBI KA MAQBARA, AURANGABAD

Aurangzeb ○   1565   AGRA FORT, AGRA

43

INDIA GOES DIGITAL

In 2016, the Digital India campaign brought internet, e-learning, online banking and digital tools to schools, cities and even remote villages. Make a list or draw five digital tools or electronic devices you use at home.

WARS THROUGH TIME

India and Pakistan have had four major wars. Complete the timeline below by filling in the year and the name of the conflict.

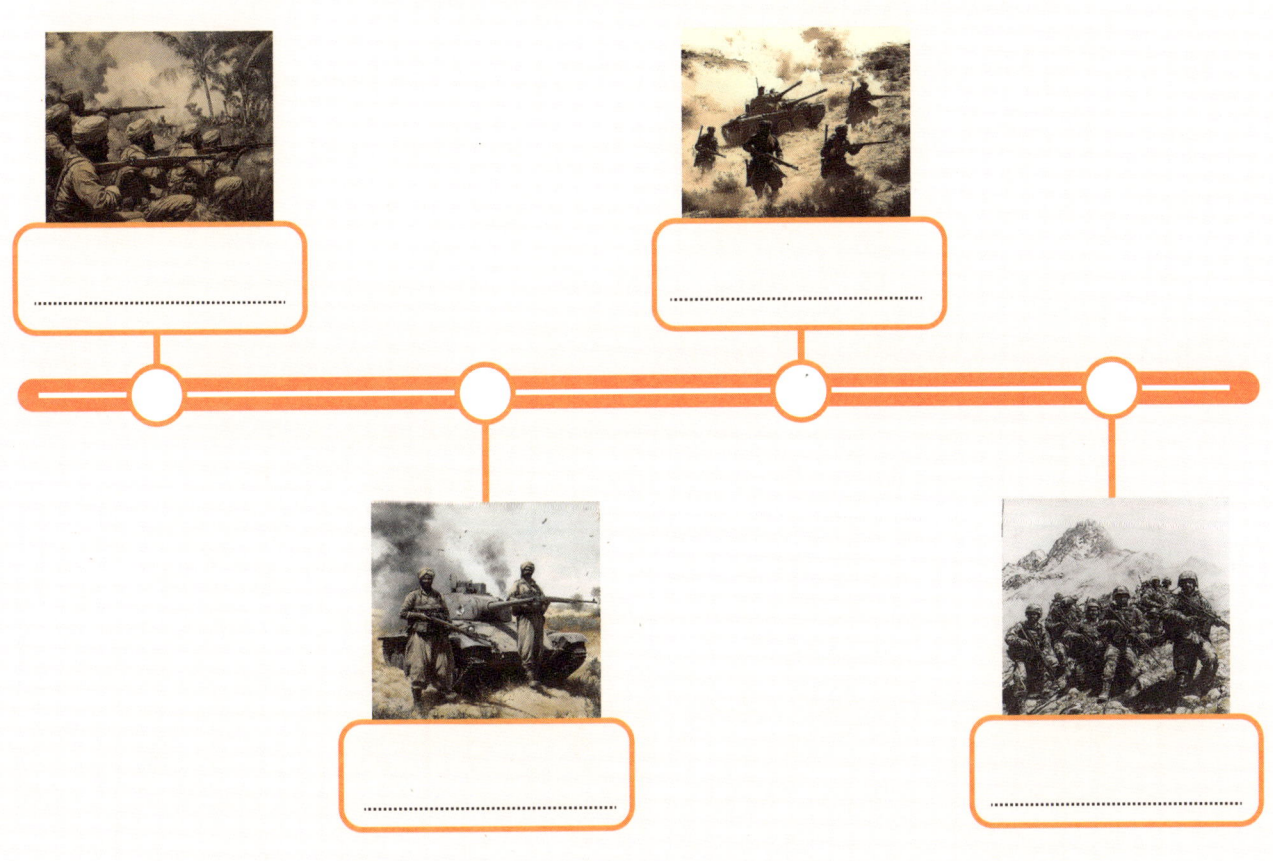

Fill in the years in the correct chronological order, from earliest to latest.

1947–48

1965

1971

1999

FREEDOM YEAR SEARCH

Hidden in the grid below are six important historical dates. Can you find them? Look vertically, horizontally and diagonally.

1857 – The First War of Independence began against British rule.

1885 – The Indian National Congress was founded.

1919 – The Jallianwala Bagh massacre shocked the nation.

1920 – The Non-Cooperation Movement was launched by Gandhi.

1930 – The Salt March began as a protest against British salt laws.

1942 – The Quit India Movement called for an end to British rule he correct year to the right event.

1	8	5	7	5	3	0	4	2	1
5	0	4	9	4	7	6	1	8	9
5	7	3	1	2	8	6	8	3	8
7	5	4	9	3	2	9	8	1	8
8	2	4	3	8	9	6	5	7	2
3	1	9	0	9	2	7	8	1	9
4	5	3	6	7	3	1	5	7	8
6	9	5	2	1	7	9	3	6	0
5	8	4	8	7	6	2	0	3	1
1	9	4	2	4	8	0	4	2	7

46

HISTORIC ADDITION

Let's use maths to explore some important years in Indian history. Solve the addition problems below and see how history adds up!

1. Aryabhatta's birth year (476) + India's Independence (1947) =

Ans..............................

2. Swami Vivekananda's birth year (1863) + Jawaharlal Nehru's birth year (1889) =

Ans..............................

3. Year of Jallianwala Bagh Massacre (1919) + Year of Quit India Movement (1942) =

Ans..............................

4. Formation of Indian National Congress (1885) + The year India won the Cricket World Cup for the first time (1983) =

Ans..............................

5. The year Rabindranath Tagore won the Nobel Prize (1913) + The year *Chandrayaan-3* landed on the Moon (2023) =

Ans..............................

BATTLE OF THE HYDASPES

In 326 BCE, Alexander the Great fought King Porus near the Hydaspes River. Despite winning, Alexander admired Porus's bravery and allowed him to remain king. Look at the image below and observe the armies on each side of the river. Circle the differences in their clothing, animals, weapons, flags and more.

DID YOU KNOW? Porus's army included 300 chariots, 30,000 infantry and 85 elephants, some equipped with armoured howdahs carrying archers and javelin men.

FIND THE SPECIAL DATE!

Hidden in this number puzzle is a big day in Indian history. Use the clues to find and circle the correct date, then write the full date.

Clues:
Happened in August (8th month).
The day is between 10 and 20
The year ends with 7 and is before 1950.
The full year uses 1, 4, 7 and one more number.

Write the date under the flag.

EMPEROR ASHOKA

Ashoka ruled during a time when years were counted backwards—from a bigger number to a smaller one! In BCE (Before Common Era), time moved toward zero. So the year 268 BCE came before 232 BCE

If Ashoka became emperor in 268 BCE and ruled until 232 BCE, how many years did he rule?

Subtract like this:

268 − 232 = _____ years

Ashoka ruled for: ____ years

Ashoka the Great	Alexander the Great	Chandragupta Maurya

268–232 BCE	336–323 BCE	321–297 BCE

Arrange the dates chronologically, starting with the oldest date and ending with the newest.

NETAJI'S BIRTHDAY NUMBER PUZZLE!

Netaji Subhas Chandra Bose was born on 23 January 1897. He became a great freedom fighter and leader. Use his birth date to solve these number puzzles!

1. How old would Netaji be today in 2025? _____

2. What do you get when you add the digits in the number 23? _____

3. Add the first and last digits of 1897. _____

4. Now, subtract the smallest digit in 1897 from the biggest one. _____

5. Write the numbers of Netaji's birthdate in order from smallest to biggest. _____

WHAT'S IT MADE OF?

On 7 August, we celebrate Indian Handloom Day to honour the weavers of India who make beautiful fabrics by hand.
Some clothes are handwoven using traditional skills. Others are machine-made in factories. Below are six clothing items.

Handwoven Fabric

◯ ◯ ◯

Machine-made Clothes

◯ ◯ ◯

1

2

3

4

5

6

THE STONE THAT MARKS AN EMPIRE

To mark the founding of the mighty Mauryan Empire, Chanakya, the chief minister to King Chandragupta Maurya, had the year carved into a stone in the royal garden. Can you spot the correct stone?

CIRCLE THE STONE!

53

THE STORY OF JAMMU AND KASHMIR

In 1947, Jammu and Kashmir was an independent state. When armed fighters from Pakistan invaded, Maharaja Hari Singh requested help from India and agreed to join the country. This led to a war that continued until 1948. Place the events in the correct order by writing 1, 2, or 3 next to each.

India sends army to help Kashmir after Maharaja joins India on 26 October 1947.

The war ends with a peace agreement on 1 January 1949.

Fighters from Pakistan enter Kashmir 22 October 1947.

MAY DAY MYSTERY NUMBERS

1 May is Labour Day—a day to celebrate and thank the hardworking people who help make our world a better place. In many parts of the world, it's also known as May Day! Some workers have left behind number clues on their toolboxes. Can you solve each equation to discover the special number they all have in common?

A farmer says: "I sow seeds in 2 fields and harvest 4 bags each. Add them up and subtract 7."
 (2 × 4) − 7 = _____

A builder says: "I made 3 walls with 2 bricks each. Then I added 1 more."
 (3 × 2) + 1 = _____

A teacher says: "You had 10 pencils. You gave away 6 and then added back 2."
 10 − 6 + 2 = _____

A doctor says: "I saw 5 patients in the morning, then 3 more, but 7 went home."
 (5 + 3) − 7 = _____

JOURNEY THROUGH TIME

Swami Vivekananda was born on 12 January 1863. He inspired many with his speeches, especially at a major event in Chicago in 1893. Since 2014, India has celebrated 12 January as National Youth Day to honour him. Here are four important years related to Swami Vivekananda's life. Can you put them in the correct order, from earliest to latest?

1863 — The year Swami Vivekananda was born

1902 — The year Swami Vivekananda passed away

2014 — The year National Youth Day started to be celebrated in his honour

1893 — The year he spoke at the Chicago World's Parliament of Religions

CRACK THE DATE

Rajaraja Chola I was a powerful ruler of the Chola Empire. He built the magnificent Brihadeeswara Temple and strengthened his kingdom, making it rich and prosperous. Solve the maths puzzle on each rock. Then, put the answers together to find out the year he became king!

THE RISE OF THE GUPTAS

Open the treasure chest to uncover the secrets of the Gupta Empire! But first, you'll need to crack the four digit secret code to unlock it. Use the clues to break the code—it includes the year the Gupta Empire began.

The first digit is the number of sides on a triangle.

The second digit is the number of wheels on a bicycle.

The third digit is the number of apples in an empty basket

The fourth digit is a sum of all the three digits.

ANSWERS

Page no : 1

Page no : 2
A - 15 August 1947
B - 26 January 1950
C - 24 September 2014
D - 2 October
E - 14 April
F - 12 March 1930

Page no : 4
1. 5 November 2013
2. 1 December 2013
3. 24 September 2014
4. 25 September 2014

Page no : 6
1. True   2. False
3. False   4. True
5. False   6. True
7. False   8. False
9. False   10. True

Page no : 7
3 sections of Wheat = 150 kg

Total Food Produced = 350 kg

5 sections of rice - 200 kg

Page no : 10

Page no : 11

Page no : 13
1. Kalpana Chawla
2. Mother Teresa
3. Indira Gandhi
4. Barkha Dutt
5. Kiran Bedi

Page no : 14
1. 6
2. 4
3. 10
4. 60
5. 6

Page no : 15
1-D
2-D
3-B
4-C
5-A

Page no : 16 & 17
1. Tamil Nadu
2. Gujarat
3. Arunachal Pradesh
4. Kerala
5. Assam
6. Madhya Pradesh

Page no : 18
INDIA

Page no : 19

Page no : 20
1. 1857
2. Mahatma Gandhi
3. Mahatma Gandhi
4. 15 August 1947

Page no : 21
Republic Day → January 26

Christmas → December 25

National Science Day → February 28

Children's Day → November 14

Makar Sankranti → January 14

Independence Day → August 15

Page no : 22 & 23
1. Agra
2. Ooty
3. Delhi
4. Pushkar
5. Kevadia
6. Varanasia

ANSWERS

Page no : 24
1-C
2-D
3-B
4-E
5-A

Page no : 25
1. 40 years
2. 58 years
3. 75 years
4. 61 years

Page no : 28
1-E
2-C
3-A
4-B
5-D

Page no : 29
1. AJMUM & KAMSHIR → JAMMU & KASHMIR
2. IKMSIK → SIKKIM
3. HPOBAL → BHOPAL
4. DYERBAHID → HYDERABAD
5. CRAVTNREOA → TRAVANCORE
6. NUJAGAD → JUNAGADH

Page no : 30
1. 1932
2. Tejas
3. Bhagavad Gita

Page no : 31

H	T	Y	K	V	R	O	V	E	R
L	O	F	E	G	Y	L	D	S	I
N	A	L	Z	T	G	O	J	D	X
I	E	R	E	D	N	A	L	N	S
T	N	A	Y	G	A	R	P	E	O
Q	M	O	O	N	O	V	G	A	R
V	I	Q	Z	Q	X	S	A	W	S
R	A	U	K	L	F	Z	Z	E	I
D	E	Q	J	U	C	N	W	X	K
H	Y	V	I	K	R	A	M	A	V

Page no : 33
1. Aviation
2. Admiral
3. Naval Base
4. Coast Guard
5. Diving
6. Submarine
7. Warship
8. Frigate

Page no : 34
1. Gudi Padwa – March/April
2. Vishu – 14 April
3. Baisakhi – 13/14 April
4. Ugadi – March/April
5. Poila Boishakh – 14/15 April

Page no : 35

I	Z	M	R	G	E	U	S	A	F
J	O	R	A	H	T	U	R	T	X
D	A	S	M	I	H	A	K	A	M
V	D	Z	U	F	A	J	N	L	W
X	M	F	P	D	M	Q	S	P	B
V	U	K	G	W	A	L	V	M	F
R	O	E	P	T	Q	Z	P	K	E
N	E	R	E	S	P	E	C	T	O
B	P	E	A	C	E	N	L	U	B
O	J	S	S	E	N	D	N	I	K

Page no : 36
1. A – Guard
2. B – Trader
3. C – Monk
4. D – Water Carrier
5. E – Scribe

Page no : 37
1. B – A farmer feeding a cow
2. D – Farmers working together with milk cans
3. C – Milk being delivered to the market
4. A – Happy families drinking fresh milk

Page no : 38
1. Qutb-ud-din Aibak (1206 CE)
2. Alauddin Khalji (1296 CE)
3. Tughlaq Dynasty (1320 CE)
4. Timur Invasion (1398 CE)
5. Babur (1526 CE)

ANSWERS

Page no : 43

1. Babur – 1526 – Aram Bagh, Agra
2. Humayun – 1570 – Humayun's Tomb, Delhi
3. Akbar – 1565 – Agra Fort, Agra
4. Shah Jahan – 1648 – Taj Mahal, Agra
5. Aurangzeb – 1678 – Bibi Ka Maqbara, Aurangabad

Page no : 45

First Indo-Pak War — 1947–48

Second Indo-Pak War — 1965

Third Indo-Pak War — 1971

Kargil War — 1999

Page no : 46

1	8	5	7	5	3	0	4	2	1
5	0	4	9	4	7	6	1	8	9
5	7	3	1	2	8	6	8	3	8
7	5	4	9	3	2	9	8	1	8
8	2	4	3	8	9	6	5	7	2
3	1	9	0	9	2	7	8	1	9
4	5	3	6	7	3	1	5	7	8
6	9	5	2	1	7	9	3	6	0
5	8	4	8	7	6	2	0	3	1
1	9	4	2	4	8	0	4	2	7

Page no : 47

1. 2423
2. 3752
3. 3861
4. 3868
5. 3936

Page no : 49

15 / 8 / 1947

Page no : 50

268 – 232 = 36

So, Ashoka ruled for 36 years.

Chronological order

336–323 BCE – Alexander the Great

321–297 BCE – Chandragupta Maurya

268–232 BCE – Ashoka the Great

Page no : 51

1. 128
2. 5
3. 8
4. 8
5. 1, 2, 3, 7, 8, 9

Page no : 52

Handwoven Fabric:
1. Saree
4. Dhoti
6. Khadi Kurta

Machine-made Clothes:
2. T-shirt
3. Uniform
5. Jeans

Page no : 53

Page no : 54

1. Fighters from Pakistan enter Kashmir: 22 October 1947.

2. India sends army to help Kashmir after Maharaja joins India: 26 October 1947.

3. The war ends with a peace agreement on 1 January 1949.

Page no : 55

Farmer : (2 × 4) − 7 = 8 − 7 = 1

Builder: (3 × 2) + 1 = 6 + 1 = 7

Teacher: 3 + 1 = 4, then add 2 → 4 + 2 = 6

Student: You had 10 pencils, gave away 6 → 10 − 6 = 4, add back 2 → 4 + 2 = 6

Doctor: (5 + 3) − 7 = 8 − 7 = 1

Page no : 56

1. 1863
2. 1893
3. 1902
4. 2014

Page no : 57

985 CE

Page no : 58

3205

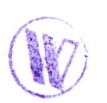